The Big Book of
Classroom Stationery

Grades 2–3

SCHOLASTIC
PROFESSIONAL BOOKS

New York • Toronto • London • Auckland • Sydney
Mexico City • New Delhi • Hong Kong • Buenos Aires

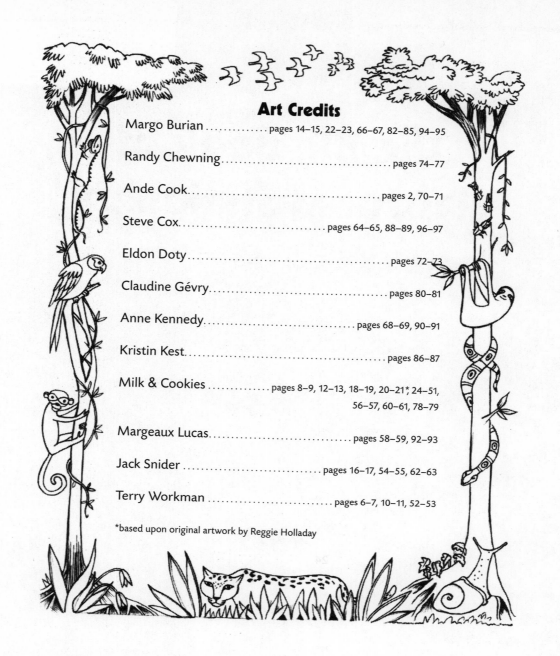

Art Credits

Margo Burian . . . . pages 14–15, 22–23, 66–67, 82–85, 94–95

Randy Chewning . . . . pages 74–77

Ande Cook . . . . pages 2, 70–71

Steve Cox . . . . pages 64–65, 88–89, 96–97

Eldon Doty . . . . pages 72–73

Claudine Gévry . . . . pages 80–81

Anne Kennedy . . . . pages 68–69, 90–91

Kristin Kest . . . . pages 86–87

Milk & Cookies . . . . pages 8–9, 12–13, 18–19, 20–21,* 24–51, 56–57, 60–61, 78–79

Margeaux Lucas . . . . pages 58–59, 92–93

Jack Snider . . . . pages 16–17, 54–55, 62–63

Terry Workman . . . . pages 6–7, 10–11, 52–53

*based upon original artwork by Reggie Holladay

Written by Kathleen Simpson
Cover design by Josué Castilleja
Cover art by Margo Burian, Milk & Cookies, and Randy Chewning
Interior design by Ampersand Design
ISBN: 0-439-42065-2

6 7 8 9 10   40   08 07

Contents

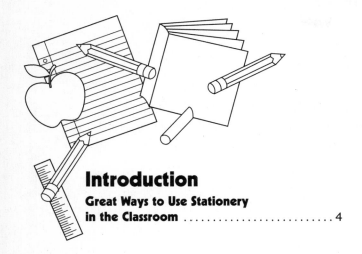

Introduction
**Great Ways to Use Stationery
in the Classroom**

Fun Shape Pages
Ruled and blank templates

Topper Pages
Track-ruled and blank templates

Months of the Year

Full Border Pages
Ruled and blank templates

Back to School

Favorite Themes and Subjects

Seasons

Special Days

Great Ways to Use Stationery in the Classroom

Are your students jazzed up about writing? Spark new ideas and offer young writers new, creative ways to express them with *The Big Book of Classroom Stationery*.

A valuable resource for any teacher, this book includes more than 85 pages of exciting stationery designs corresponding to classroom themes, seasons, special days, and months of the year. Lined and unlined shapes, toppers, and borders are great for showcasing both writing and artwork. Pages are perforated for easy removal and photocopying.

You and your students will find countless ways to make learning fun with these stationery designs. Here are a few ideas to get you started.

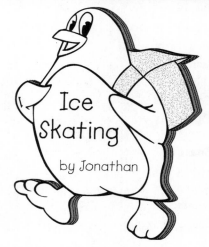

Ice Skating by Jonathan

Create Shape Books With Shape Stationery or Toppers

Choose a stationery design that's appropriate for each student's story—for example, you might use the Mitten or Penguin design for a story about a wintry day. Make multiple copies of the selected pages. Let students cut out several pages of the same design and staple these pages together to create a shape booklet that frames their writing.

Personalize Journals

Make a class set of copies of 20–30 stationery designs. Invite children to choose an assortment of these designs and then staple them together (or use a three-hole punch and a three-ring binder) to make a personalized journal. Encourage students to color in borders with markers and to add different designs as the journals begin to fill out. As the year progresses, offer choices of new designs.

Festive Displays of Students' Work

The Best Thing About Fall

Fall is a great season, because I get to play soccer every week!

To create two-sided hanging shapes using the symmetrical shape borders (Birthday Cake, Star, Valentine, Pencil, and Butterfly) give students two copies each of the same shape design. Have students write on one sheet of shape stationery and color in or paint the second sheet. Cut out both shapes and staple or glue them back-to-back. For asymmetrical shapes (Apple, Pumpkin, Bus, Mitten, and Penguin), have students design and cut out one sheet only. They can create a colorful back for their work by tracing the shape facedown onto construction paper. Attach yarn or string to the tops so the decorated shapes can hang from the ceiling or dangle from the top of a bulletin board. Viewers can browse and flip them to appreciate the artwork and the writing.

Current Events

Challenge students to write about current events, both those in the news and events that affect them on a personal level. By recording information on the appropriate Months of the Year topper, students can keep a record of events over the course of a year that they can easily sort by month. These pages can become part of each child's personalized journal.

Frame Poetry and Art With Borders

Invite students to compose poetry, polish it, and then create a final copy on border stationery. To show off their artwork, trim around students' pictures and glue them in the middle of the border "frames." Students can color in the borders for a unique look.

Send Letters Home

Use eye-catching stationery to send a special thank-you note to that hardworking volunteer. Use Months of the Year toppers to send home calendars with upcoming events in the classroom, or to keep families up to date on your curriculum.

Announce Special Occasions

Encourage children to cut out the Birthday Cake design and compose their birthday wishes, use the Thanksgiving page to deliver holiday greetings, or announce the first year's snowfall with the Weather page.

Coordinate With Classroom Themes

Doing a unit on transportation? Students can write about their experiences with buses, trains, and cars on the Transportation page. Studying butterflies? Have them use Butterfly stationery to write about migrating monarchs or a butterfly emerging from its cocoon. The Multicultural Kids border can help set the stage for learning about students' families as well as cultures around the world.

Accordion Books

Lay sheets of stationery so they alternate back-to-back and front-to-front. Next, tape the sides together at the back of the page to create an accordion book. What a delightful way to display students' writing!

Inspire Young Writers With Story Starters

Invite students to choose a stationery design and then have them write a story, poem, or article related to the design they've chosen. Money and Time might inspire a story about saving for a special gift, while Dinosaurs might help a young writer produce an article about Tyrannosaurus Rex.

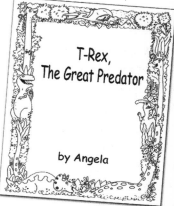

Create Award Certificates

Use stationery to create certificates that recognize hard work or positive behavior. Send home a "Star Award" with the star shape page for special effort, kindness, or creativity. Use Months of the Year designs to congratulate children for completing a unit of study or to recognize "Helpers of the Month."

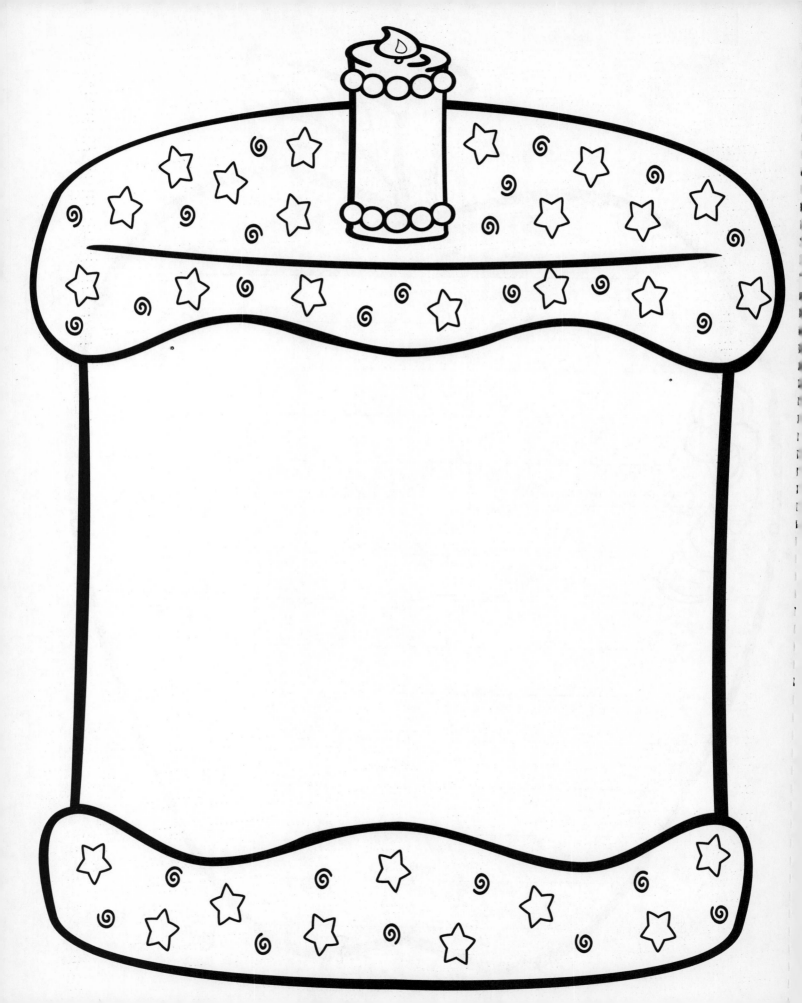

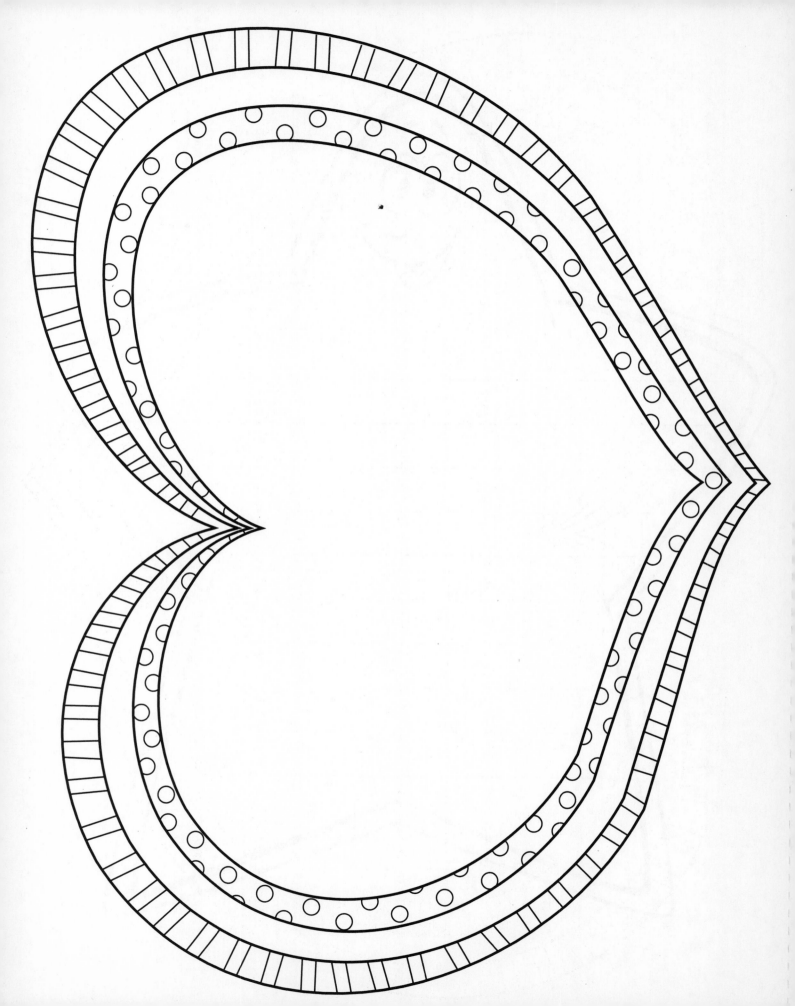

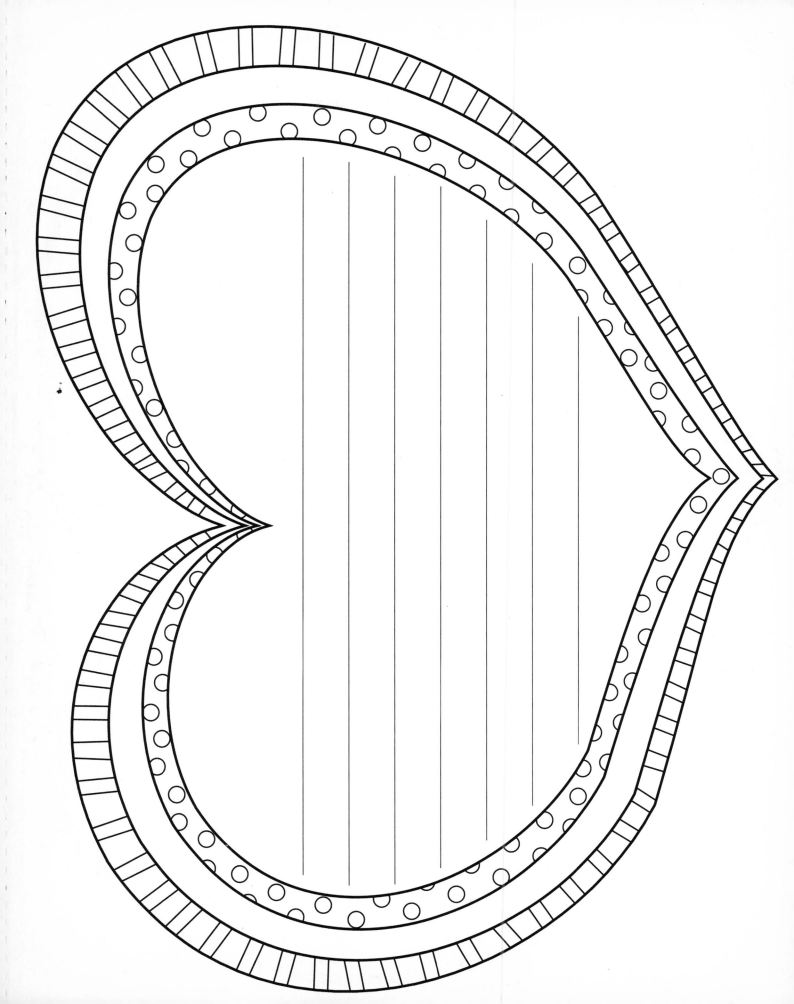

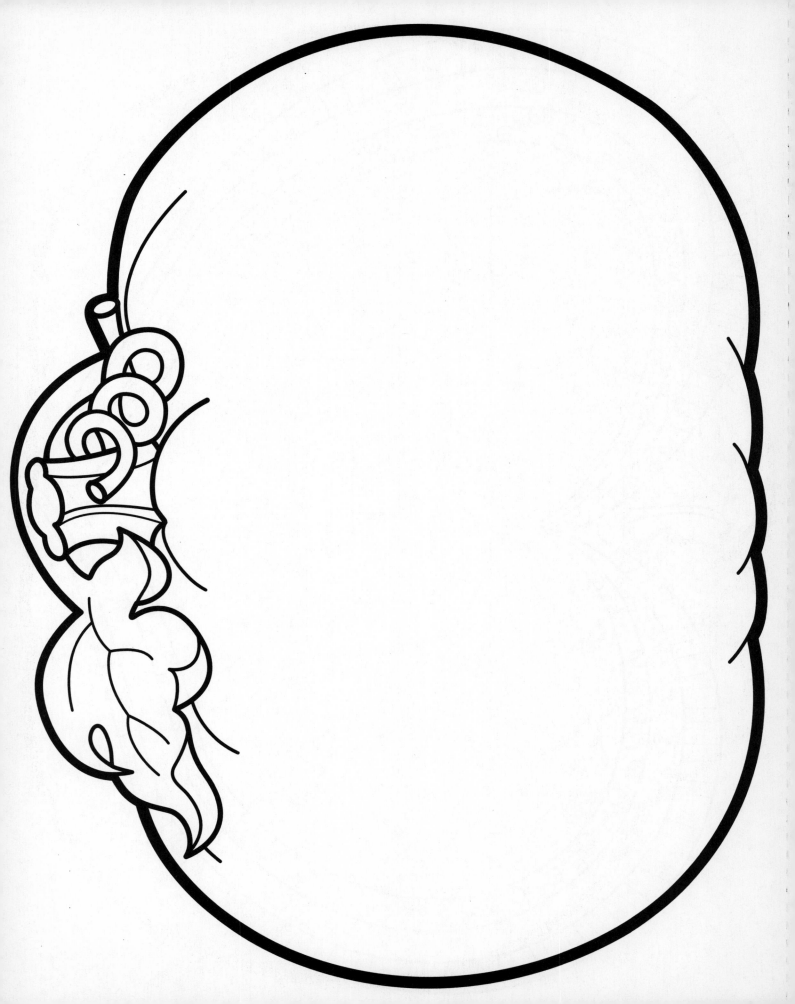

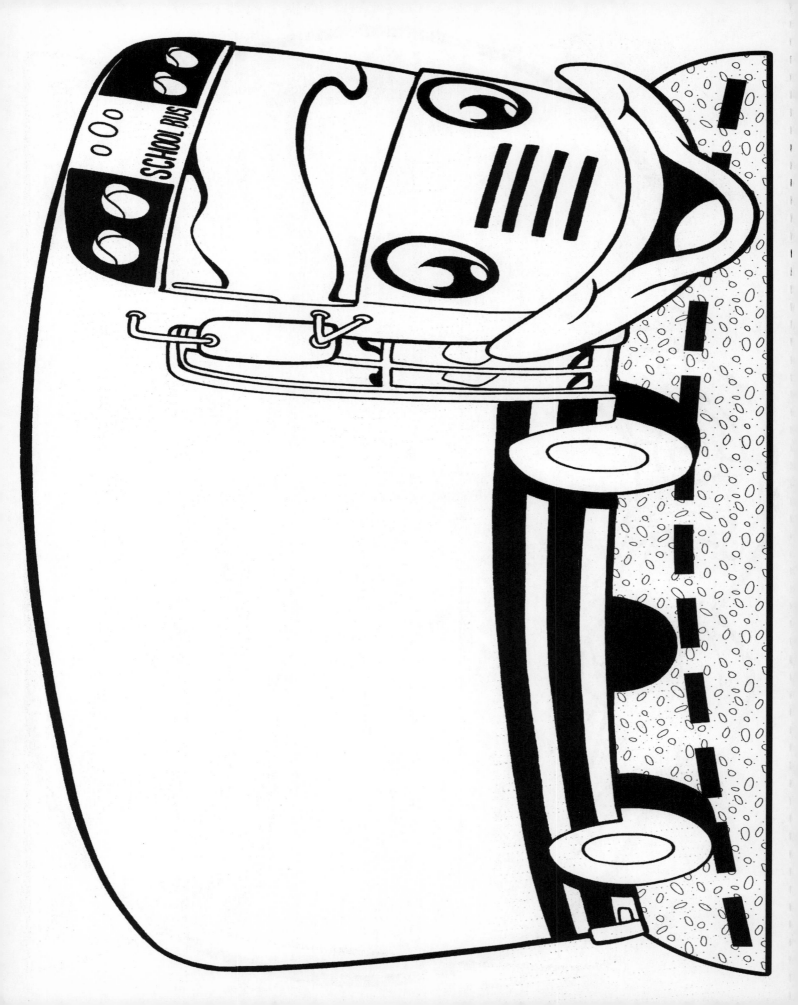

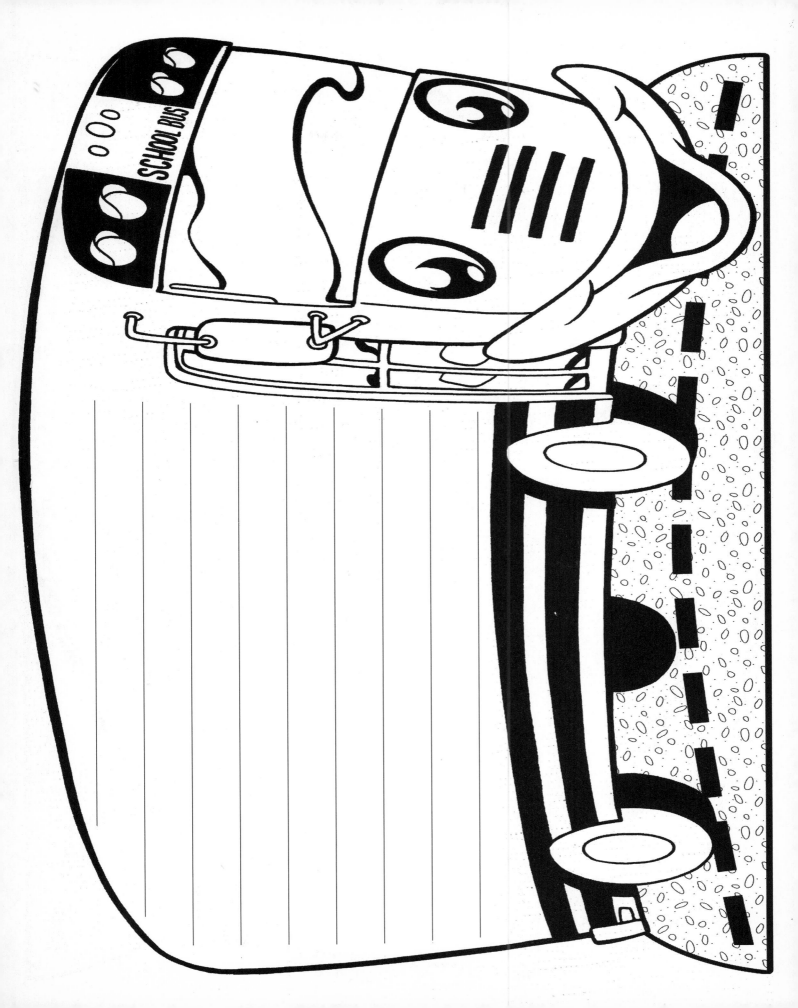

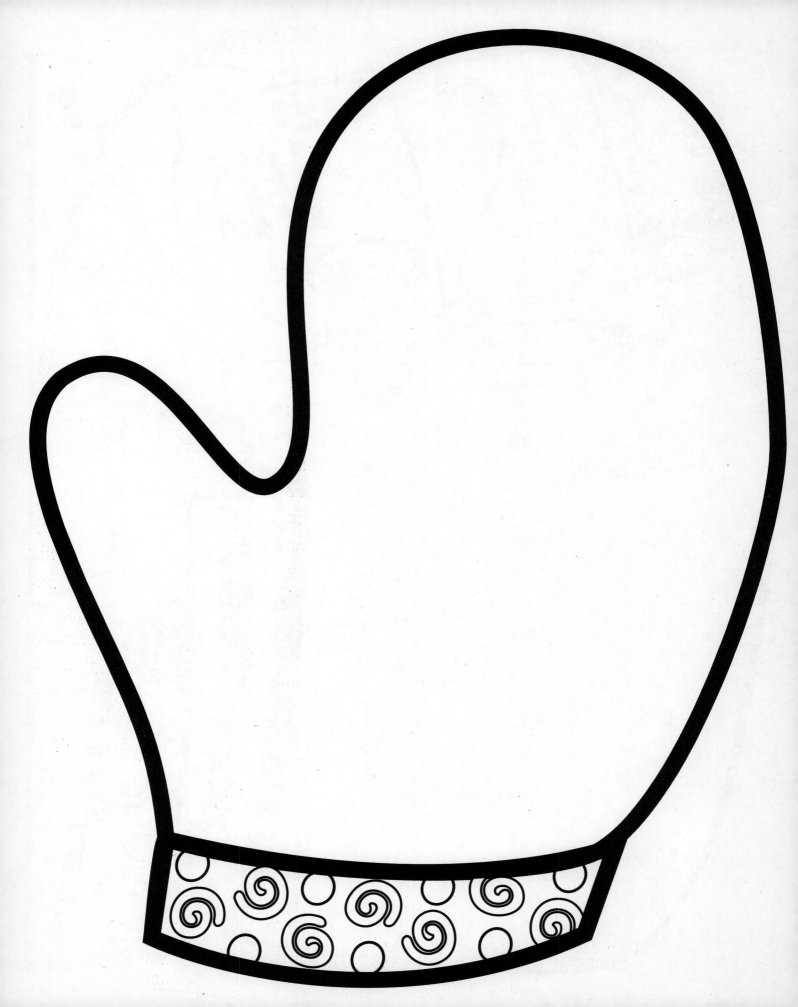

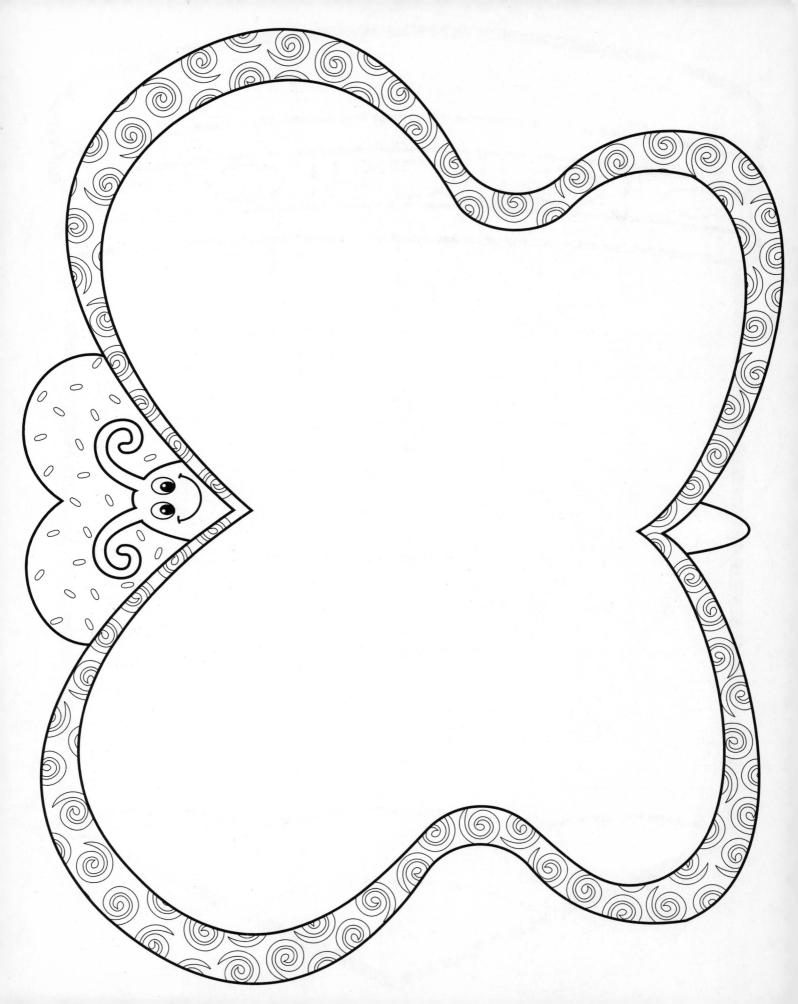

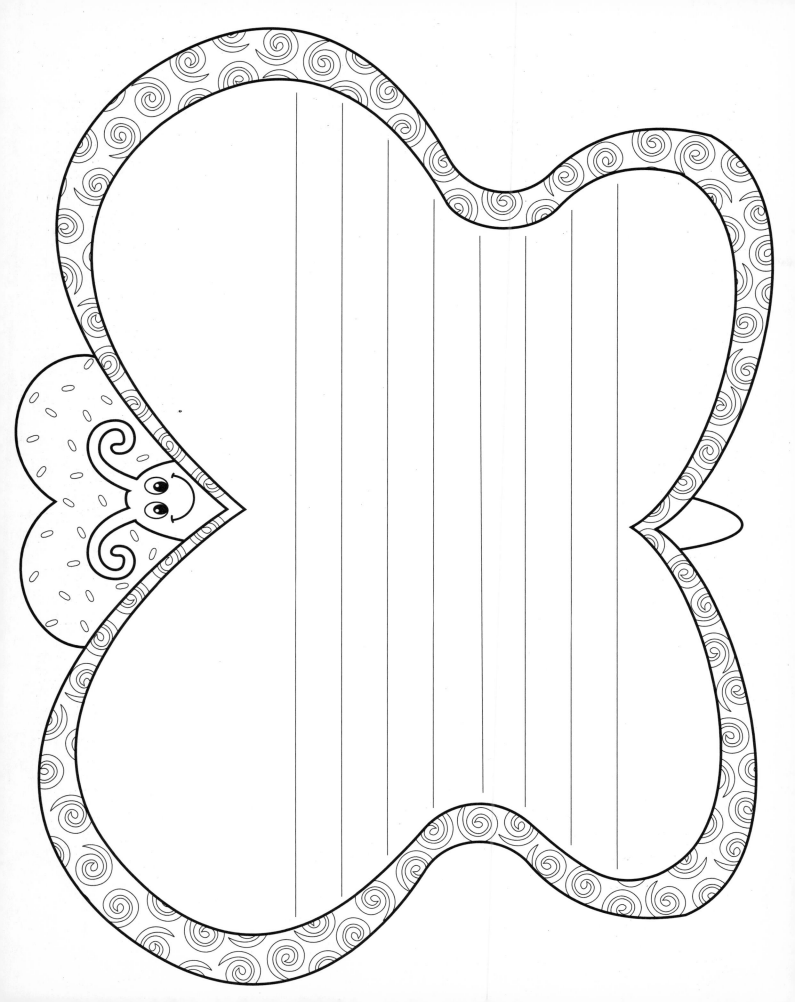

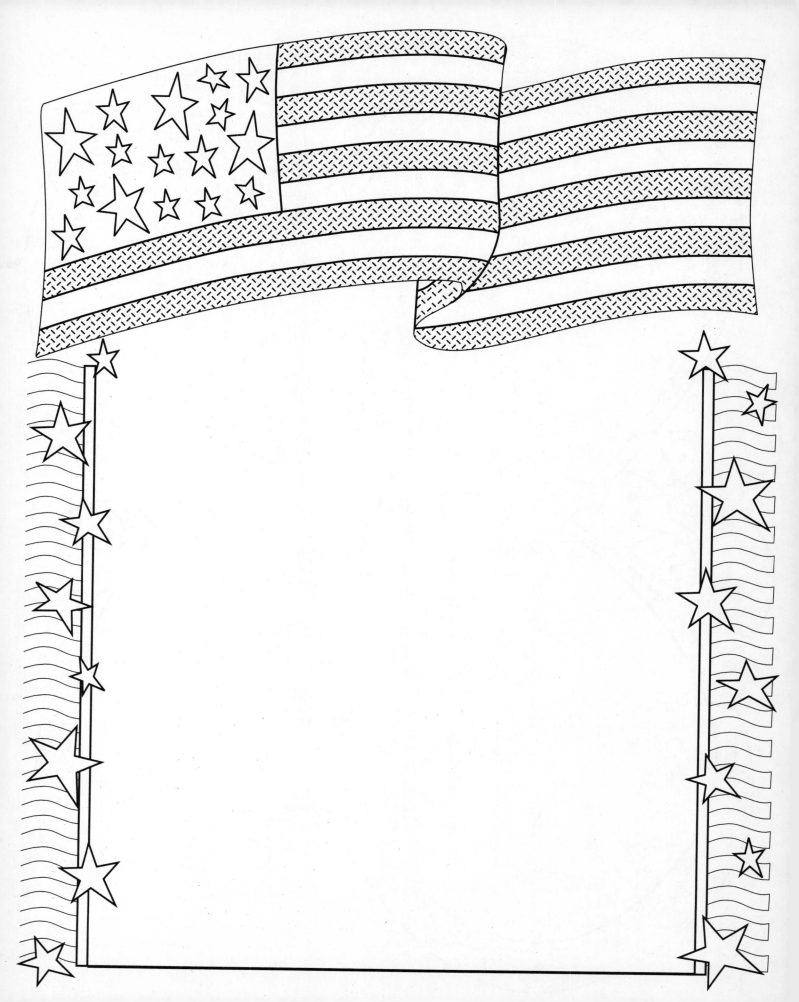

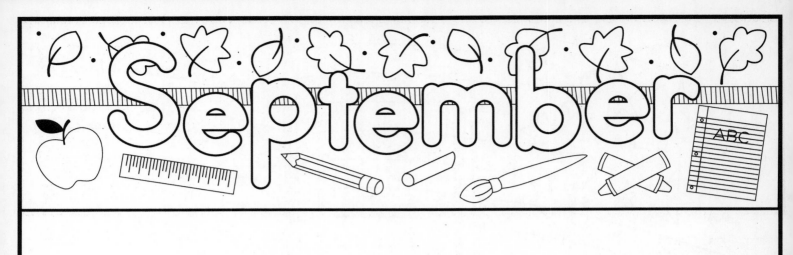

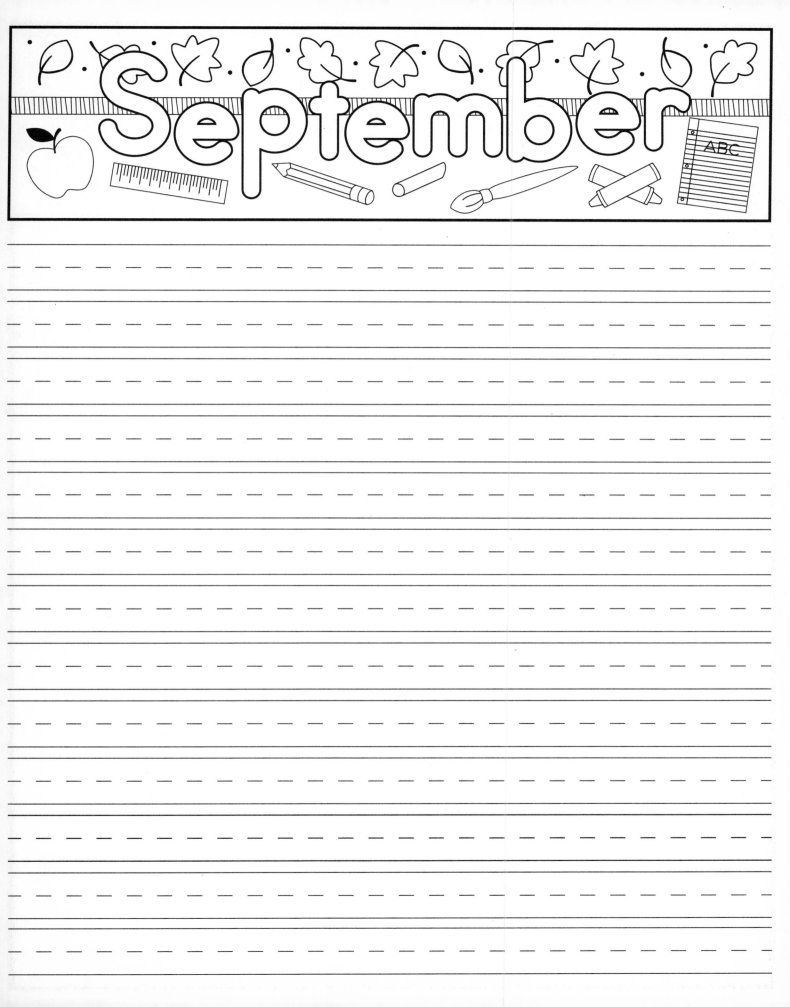

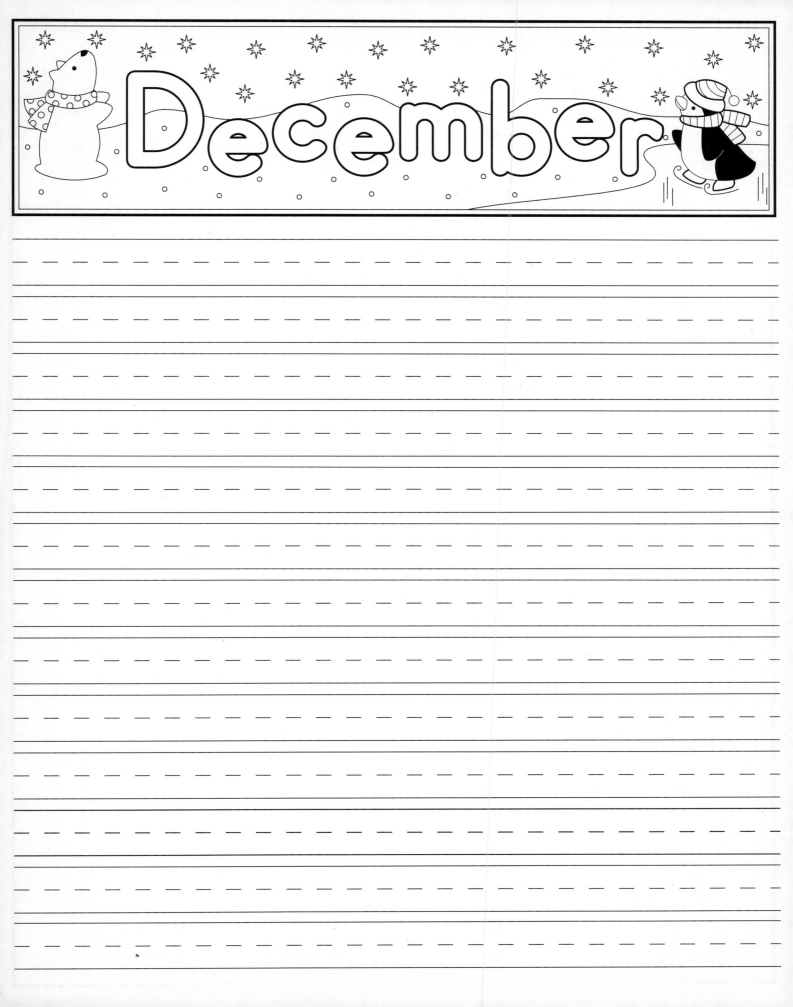

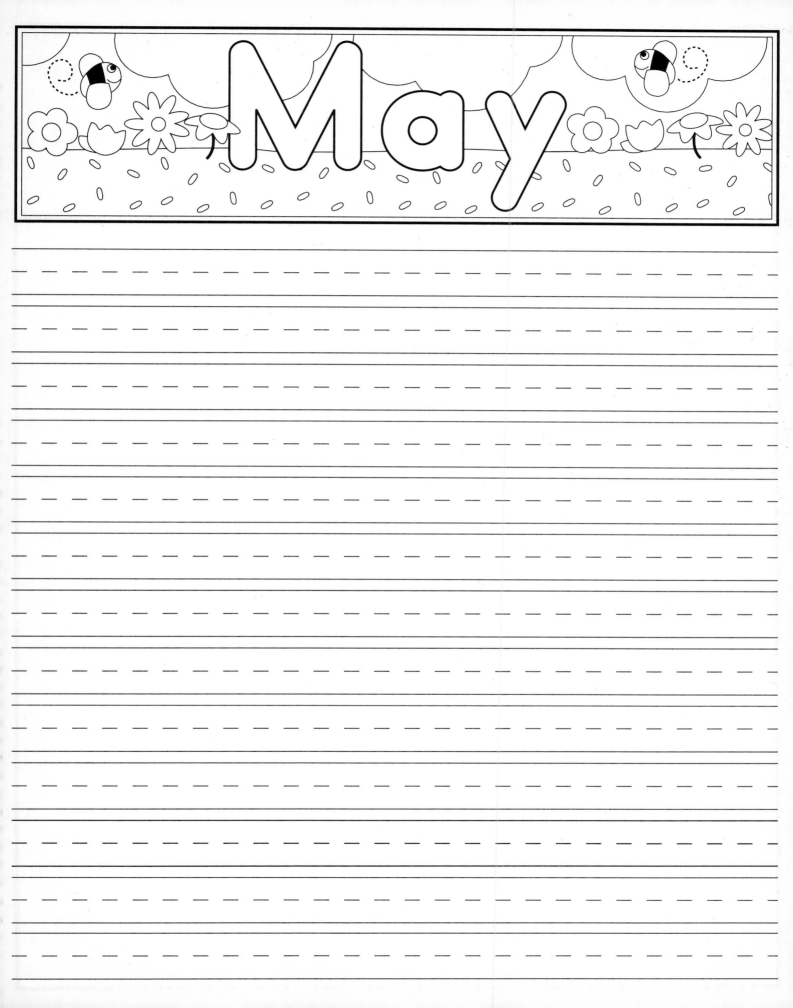

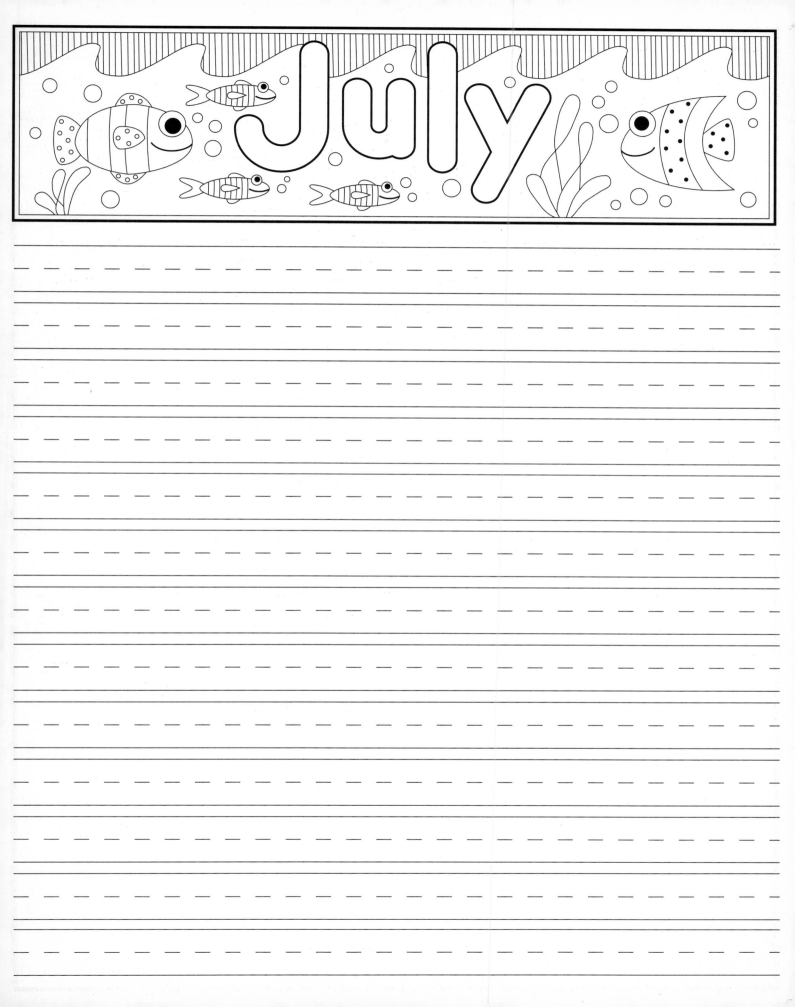

Vv Ww Xx Yy Zz Aa

Uu Bb

Tt Cc

Ss Dd

Rr Ee

Qq Ff

Pp Gg

Oo Hh

Nn Mm Ii Jj Kk Ll

WASHINGTON

LINCOLN

WASHINGTON   LINCOLN